HANDCRAFTED COCKTAILS

The Mixologist's Guide to Classic Drinks
for Morning, Noon & Night

Molly Wellmann

BETTERWAY HOME
CINCINNATI, OHIO
WWW.BETTERWAYBOOKS.COM

CONTENTS

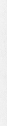

CHAPTER 5: HAPPY HOUR DRINKS   98

INTRODUCTION

THIS BOOK IS WHAT MY BAR, JAPP'S, IS ALL ABOUT. Japp's is the kind of bar I want to spend time in. Although there are many fine drinking establishments in Cincinnati, I couldn't find any that had a feeling of stepping back in time. It seemed that each bar I entered contained a conversation-killing television that continually flashed ESPN in patrons' faces. I don't know why, but to me, televisions in bars seem cheap and kind of rude. I wanted a place that presented an entirely new bar experience for twenty-first century patrons by creating an environment that referenced a bygone time when people drank and socialized at a bar without needing to scream to be heard.

I wanted a place where the only thing that diverted a good conversation was catching a glance of a hot Tomato or a gorgeous sheik of a man (but not in the commercial on television).

I also wanted the drinks to reflect the same quality as those made a hundred years ago, when bartenders used quality, fresh ingredients and balanced the flavors instead of making them too sweet. I was sick of ordering cocktails made from cheap, artificially flavored, neon-colored liqueurs made with high-fructose corn syrup that left a chemical aftertaste. I wanted a place where I could get a well-balanced drink that was carefully crafted by a bartender

who could tell me more about the spirits I was about to enjoy. I wanted a place where the bartender would showcase new liquors on the shelf and sell me on what made that liquor so special.

So Japp's was born.

DRINK IN SOME KNOWLEDGE

I'm obsessed with cocktails and spirits. I always say that I'm a weird kind of alcoholic. I find the stories about the liquor as intoxicating as the drinks themselves. I drink in as much knowledge about spirits and cocktails as I can until I'm giddy…but I can still drive at the end of that experience. And I don't have to go to rehab yet. (I'm secretly kind of a lightweight. When I do drink, I can

handle only about three drinks in a night before I'm a little bit loopy.) I love to learn the stories about where everything comes from. I always have.

Alcohol has had its hand in almost every part of civilized history. Humans have been drinking beer and wine since before 8,000 B.C. and distilled spirits since around 800 B.C. The fermentation process is believed to have been discovered by accident. Someone left some water in some grain, forgot about it for a few days, and then drank. The resulting beverage made the drinker feel good. According to legend, wine was discovered more than eight thousand years ago in Persia, during the reign of the great king Jamshid. It was a time of great discoveries that made life

easier and more enjoyable. The legend goes that the king banished a woman from his harem. This woman was so devastated that she decided suicide was the only answer to the pain she was  feeling. So she went to the king's warehouses and found a jar marked poison. The jar contained spoiled grapes that were thought to be undrinkable and poisonous. In reality, the grapes hadn't spoiled. They had been broken down by the yeast in the air and fermented. After drinking the fermented grape juice, the woman felt light and elated. She took the discovery back to the king, who loved it. He let the woman back into his harem and declared that from that day forward, all the grapes were to be used to make wine.

The Chinese started distilling fermented rice to create rice wine. The distilling process spread, and people began using it with grapes to create wine. In areas where grapes didn't grow, people would distill grain to make alcohol. Not all distillers were seeking libations. Some believed distilling wine would make gold. Others used the distilling process to make perfume or medicine.

People have been mixing herbs, fruit, and sugar into their alcohol since they started to drink distilled spirits, mostly to cover up the harsh flavors of the liquor, but also for medicinal purposes. For instance, the gin and tonic comes from the British sailors' practice of mixing their quinine, which was horribly bitter, with their ration of gin and a bit of sugar. The lime was added to prevent scurvy. The distilling and fermentation process also kills harmful microbes found in water, making it safer to drink a distilled or fermented

drink rather than the water, especially in densely populated areas where sanitation was minimal to non-existent, and cholera and dysentery were real threats carried in drinking water.

Bartenders began writing down recipes for mixed drinks and creating reference guides for making drinks starting in the nineteenth century. Jerry Thomas was the first to do this, publishing *The Bar-Tender's Guide* in 1862. Before Thomas's guide, bartenders learned new drinks from travelers who asked for mixed drinks they'd had at a bar in another city they had passed through.

Here in Cincinnati, Christopher F. Lawlor was the best bartender in town in the late 1800s. He tended bar at a few local establishments (and in those days, there were quite a few—more than 1,800 saloons in downtown) including The Grand Hotel, which was located on Fourth and Central, before becoming the chief bartender at the Burnet House, one of the city's grandest hotels operating from 1850–1926. During his time at the Burnet House, Lawlor earned the nickname "The Prince of Mixologists" and rose to national acclaim in the 1890s. He worked special parties around the city, edited a newsletter about wine and spirits, and wrote a cocktail book entitled *The Mixicologist: or How to Mix All Kinds of Fancy Drinks: An Up-To-Date Recipe Book*. It was the first cocktail book written in Cincinnati and one of only sixteen cocktail books in print when it was released in 1895. The book is packed with the best cocktails, punches, and

The Burnet House, where Christopher F. Lawlor rose to national acclaim.

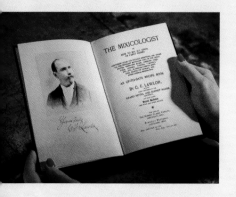

even "tempest" drinks of the time. It includes recipes that are unique to Cincinnati, such as the Cincinnati cocktail and the Spificator, which is basically a highball (but I'll always call it a Spificator!). The book is even more fascinating because it's packed with advertisements for businesses in and around Cincinnati during the 1890s. At the turn of the twentieth century, Lawlor exited the bartending business in favor of publishing and moved to Cleveland. He's buried on the west side of Cincinnati. Though I own many cocktail books, *The Mixicologist* is by far my favorite, and I'm proud to be following in Lawlor's footsteps by writing the second cocktail book to come out of Cincinnati and by making drinks that I feel both you, my reader, and my Cincinnati patrons can enjoy for a long time to come.

While delving into the history for all the cocktails included in this book, I found many interesting stories, one more fascinating than the next. The ones I've chosen are those that I found most fascinating. Are the stories true? I have no reason to believe they aren't, but because I wasn't there to verify every fact, we will have to rely on my research and the details it uncovered.

You may wonder why I felt it important to pour over stacks of old cocktail history and mixology books written by other cocktail historians in order to gather the stories contained in this book. First of all, I have great respect for those who wrote the books, and second, I have an insatiable desire to learn. In looking into the

background of the cocktails, I am able to convey to you, my reader, history that will make your next cocktail an experience rather than just a drink. As you sip your manhattan, Sazerac, or martini, you can travel back to the time when this drink was first popular and understand why people loved it.

I have adjusted ingredients in some of the cocktail recipes for several reasons. I like to have balance in a drink. I also like a drink made with only fresh ingredients. One of my signatures is my use of syrups, bitters, and juices that I've made fresh myself.

It's important to know that it's very unlikely that the drink ingredients that were used a century ago are anything like the ingredients available today. I have re-created the vintage cocktails in this book using today's ingredients and attempted to bring the drinks as close to the originals as possible. Considering the fact that Ohio is a controlled state, and Ohio is where I mix cocktails, finding just the right ingredient can sometimes be a challenge.

So let's get started on our trip down memory lane. I hope that you find this an enlightening and most pleasant journey.

Cheers!

Molly Wellmann
Cincinnati, Ohio

1

BARTENDING TOOLS AND TECHNIQUES

I SEE BARTENDING AS AN ART FORM for all of the senses. It starts with an entertaining visual presentation and ends with a delicious combination of spirits and flavors. The right presentation turns a cocktail into an experience, and that's what drinking should be about—the experience.

Mixologists should always remember that whenever they are behind a bar, they are bartenders first. The difference between a mixologist and a bartender is that a mixologist takes bartending one step further. The bartender tends the bar, making sure everyone has a drink and the drinks are rung up and the bar is clean and taken care of. Mixologists are knowledgeable of everything on the back of the bar. They know how the spirits are made, where they come from, and what to do with them. And in addition to serving (and knowing the history of) the classics, they invent new drinks.

Bartenders should be friendly, approachable, and knowledgeable. They're not order takers; they are friendly salespeople ready to suggest something new for the guest to try—something the patron may have never had before but will crave in the future. Remember the first time you tasted your favorite drink? Something about that experience keeps you coming back to that drink. As a mixologist, I want to turn you onto something new to crave, and

hopefully it includes a great backstory to complete the experience. Many of the recipes in this book include the drink's backstory that will help enhance the experience of your guests (whether they're guests at your home or paying customers at your establishment).

When it comes to making drinks, my philosophy is to balance the sweet, the sour, and the bitter along with the complementing spirit so the end result is interesting but not too sweet.

BARTENDING TOOLS

Whether you're a professional bartender or setting up a home bar, using the right equipment makes it quick and easy to mix a great cocktail every time. You can find these tools online or in higher-end kitchen stores or department stores.

Muddler: A muddler is a small, bat-shaped stick similar to a pestle that is used with a mortar, but it is longer so it fits into a mixing glass. I like to use a wooden muddler with a smooth end instead of a stainless steel muddler because the wood doesn't scratch the glass or rip the fruit apart too much.

Jigger: A jigger is an hourglass-shaped stainless steel cup with one end that is larger than the other. The larger end typically holds 1½ ounces (a standard shot), and the small end holds a smaller amount (½ ounce). A jigger is essential for quick and easy measuring.

Bartending tools. 1. cocktail strainers; 2. jigger; 3. Boston shaker mixing glass; 4. channel knife; 5. muddler; 6. barspoons; 7. Boston shaker tin

Cocktail Shaker: There are a few different kinds of shakers. The two most common are the cobbler and the Boston. Cobbler shakers consist of three stainless steel parts that fit together: a mixing tin, a top with holes in it, and a cap that covers the holes as you

shake. Boston shakers have two parts: a tin and a mixing glass that fits inside the tin. We use Boston shakers at Japp's.

Cocktail Strainer: A cocktail strainer is a stainless steel disc that has holes in it and is connected to a handle. Most of the disc is edged with a spring that helps seal the strainer to a cocktail shaker or mixing glass.

Bar Spoon: Bar spoons have very long (about 11 inches), twisted handles (the twists enhance the spoon's stirring abilities). In addition to stirring, bar spoons can also be used for measuring. They hold a teaspoon (5ml) of liquid.

Channel Knife: Channel knives are specifically designed to create twists. They are easy to guide and cut right through citrus rinds.

Bar Mat: Bar mats are made of black rubber. Always mix and pour over a bar mat. They provide a stable, slip-free surface for mixing, while containing spills and protecting the bar top.

Glassware

Each recipe in this book tells you the type of glass used to serve the drink. Here's a list and brief description of the glasses used:

Cocktail Glass (also called a coupe): is stemmed and shallow with a wide rim

Champagne Flute: is stemmed and tall with a narrow rim

Highball Glass: is straight, tall, and has a narrow diameter

Old Fashioned Glass: is short with a wide diameter

Rocks Glass: is shorter than an old fashioned glass but has the same wide diameter

Mug: features heat-resistant glass with a handle

Glassware. 1. cocktail glass (coupe); 2. highball glass; 3. rocks glass; 4. mug; 5. champagne flute; 6. old fashioned glass

BARTENDING TECHNIQUES

Muddling

Muddling means to smash or crush, and it's a technique used to release more flavor from fresh fruits, vegetables, or herbs (such as mint) in a cocktail. Muddling releases juice and oils from the fruits' and vegetables' skins and releases the essence of herbs. To muddle, place your ingredients in a mixing glass and smash or crush them with a muddler.

Measuring

One of the key ways to achieve a balanced cocktail is to measure. We're able to create great-tasting cocktails at Japp's because we

Muddling

Measuring

measure! Our bartending measuring tool of choice is a jigger. We use a 1½ to 2 ounce pour in the majority of our cocktails. When it comes to measuring, a good rule of thumb is to not measure over the glass but a bit to the side so if the spirit overflows, the excess doesn't end up in the glass. (Measure over a bartending mat for easy cleanup.) Accurate measurements ensure all of the ingredients in a cocktail work together to create a delicious drink experience. Subtle flavor complements are easily lost or overpowered when too much of any ingredient is added.

Pouring

Pouring, like measuring, is important to achieve a well-balanced cocktail. There's no need to overpour, and no one is crazy about an underpour. Also, a proper pouring technique will make you faster so you can serve more drinks. Here's the technique: Hold the neck of the bottle so you have control. Place your thumb on the base of the pour spout so it is secure and then turn the bottle over to pour.

Shaking

Shaking is a big thing for me. I get so discouraged when I order a drink and the bartender haphazardly shakes it, like he's thinking *Oh, God, I can't believe this girl ordered a drink that makes me take the extra time to shake it*. If you're a bartender, you should enjoy making drinks for people, and you should look like you enjoy it! A proper shaking technique makes customers more excited about their drink orders and shows them you care about what you do. I like to mix everything in the mixing glass in front of my customers so they can see the process and everything that is going into

Pouring   **Shaking**

the drink. I add all the ingredients first and then add the ice right before I'm about to shake it so the ice doesn't have a chance to melt and water down the drink.

After you have added everything that needs to be shaken, place the shaking tin on the glass at an angle and give the top a firm tap. This should seal the tin to the glass (get a good seal or you'll have a mess on your hands when you start shaking).

Hold the mixing glass in one hand and the tin in the other hand so they are firmly pressed together.

Turn the shaker so the opening of the shaking tin is pointed away from the customer. The opening of the shaker should never be facing your customer or your ice well just in case your seal isn't as strong as you thought. (You might get a cocktail shower, but

Stirring

Making a twist

better you than your guest, and it's better than the glass falling into your ice and having to burn the whole well.)

Hold the shaker up over your shoulder and shake vigorously. (Never shake low, in front of your body—it just doesn't look good. Get your arms up and give your guest a show.) Between ten and fifteen shakes should do it, depending on what kind of drink you're making. (Most important, smile while you shake! We are so lucky to have such a cool job!)

After you finish shaking, hold the mixing glass and the tin in one hand with the mixing glass on top and the tin on the bottom. Place your hand where the mixing glass is tilted outward. With your other hand, slap the spot where the glass and the tin meet inward. This should release the seal, and all the liquid, ice, and

ingredients should be in the tin. Don't ever tap on the bar—it looks bad and will ruin both your tin and your bar top.

Place the strainer over the tin and pour the drink into the appropriate serving glass. Shaking takes some practice, but once you've got it, you've got it!

Stirring

When you are preparing a drink that is all alcohol (such as a classic martini), it's better to stir the drink rather than shake it. Stirring properly chills the drink while maintaining a soft feel in the mouth. It also keeps your drink crystal clear. A shaken drink becomes cloudy, and the liquor takes on a sharper feel in the mouth. The proper stirring technique is to put all the ingredients in the mixing glass, add ice, and use a stirrer or bar spoon to stir. For stability, hold the top of the glass as you stir.

Making a Twist

At Japp's, we garnish a lot of our drinks with twists, usually from a lemon or an orange. The citrus peel has aromatic oils that delicately transform a drink and add a bit of freshness without the bite. We cut fresh twists for every drink as it's made. The easiest way to make a twist is with a channel knife or a zester. The trick is to let your thumb guide the channel knife and be careful! Again, practice makes perfect.

2

SPIRITS, HANDCRAFTED MIXERS, AND MORE

WHEN IT COMES TO MAKING DRINKS, my philosophy is to balance the sweet, the sour, and the bitter along with the complementing spirit so the end result is interesting but not too sweet. One way we accomplish this balance at Japp's is by making our own ingredients. We make everything from simple syrups to house-made liqueurs to cordials to bitters to tinctures to vermouths to squeezing fresh juices every day. Because we make our own ingredients, the sky is the limit on the drinks we can come up with. I'm not big on infusing entire bottles of vodka. I think you have a lot more flexibility by making a drink to complement what the distillers have already done.

The recipes in this book will yield the best results if you handcraft your own ingredients by following the instructions in this chapter.

SPIRITS

The recipes in each chapter are organized by the main spirit used in the cocktail. Inferior ingredients will produce an inferior cocktail. Whenever possible, choose a high-quality brand of liquor. It will make all the difference. If a particular brand of liquor is noted in a recipe, use that brand because the other ingredients were selected to work with that particular spirit. You won't get the same balance of flavors if you use a different brand.

Here's a quick description of the spirits used, along with some brand recommendations.

Whiskey: Whiskey is distilled from mash, but a wide variety of grains can be used, including barley, rye, wheat, and corn. It has a light, caramel, oaky flavor. Two brands I recommend are Powers Irish Whiskey and Old Grand-Dad Bonded.

Rye: By law, American rye whiskey is distilled from a mash made of at least 51 percent rye. It has a spicy flavor. Two brands I recommend are Old Overholt and Russell's Reserve Rye.

Bourbon: Bourbon is an American whiskey distilled from a mash made of at least 51 percent corn. It has a heavenly flavor that includes vanilla and oak with sweet and spicy notes. I recommend Bulleit Bourbon and Old Forester Bourbon for mixing cocktails.

Scotch: Scotch is a whisky made in Scotland. It must be aged in oak barrels for at least three years. Two brands I recommend are Dewar's and Wild Scotsman.

Rum: Rum is distilled from either molasses or sugarcane juice. It has a sweet, floral flavor. Two brands I recommend are 10 Cane and Bacardi.

Gin: Gin gets its distinct flavor from juniper berries. With gin

especially, it's important to select a good brand. The wrong one can turn a person off to gin for life. Two brands I recommend are Plymouth Gin and Watershed Distillery Gin.

Vodka: Although it can be made from potatoes, most vodkas today are grain based. I recommend Buckeye Vodka and OYO Vodka. Both brands are made in Ohio.

Tequila: Tequila is distilled from the blue agave plant. It has a sweet, cool, "green" flavor. Two brands I recommend are Cazadores and Ocho Tequila.

Brandy: Brandy is made by distilling wine. Two brands I recommend are Rémy Martin VSOP and Hennessy VSOP.

Sherry: Sherry is a fortified wine. We use Sandeman brand sherry at Japp's.

Champagne: Champagne is a type of sparkling white wine that ranges in flavor from dry to sweet. For the cocktails in this book, I recommend a mumm cuvée champagne such as Moët.

LIQUEURS AND CORDIALS

Liqueurs and cordials are flavored spirits that are sweetened when bottled. Their history stretches back centuries, when they were commonly made by monks for medicinal use. At Japp's, we use a lot of the very old classic liqueurs, such as Licor 43, Bénédictine, whose recipe dates back to the 1500s, and Chartreuse from the 1600s (yes, the liqueur's distinct green color inspired the color of the same name). We also use some liqueurs developed in the 1800s, including Luxardo Maraschino and Grand Marnier, along with some quality newer ones from the twentieth century, St. Germain and Domaine de Canton.

But we do make some of our own. I like to make falernum (pronounced fah-learn-um), which has a spicy ginger, almond, and rum flavor. It originated in the Caribbean islands in the 1700s and was a popular mixer in many tiki drinks during the 1930s.

I also make my own lime cordial, similar to the Rose's brand lime juice cordial, which was created in response to the Merchant Shipping Act of 1867. The act required British sailors to take a regular, specifically prescribed ration of lime juice to prevent scurvy. The cordial was a more enjoyable way to take the ration, and it soon caught on with the general public as well.

FALERNUM

This is my version of falernum. It's usually made with almond extract, but I use vanilla extract.

1 bottle white rum
1 cup sliced ginger
Zest from 8 limes
12 cloves
12 allspice berries
3 sticks of cinnamon
8 star anise
½ cup vanilla extract
2 cups simple syrup (give or take to taste)
Gallon glass jar with lid

In a gallon-sized glass jar add rum, ginger, lime zest, cloves, all-spice berries, cinnamon sticks, and star anise. Let sit twenty-four hours. Strain and add vanilla and simple syrup. Bottle.

LIME CORDIAL

1 cup sugar
1 cup water
Zest from 3 limes

Add all the ingredients to a pot over medium heat. Stir constantly as you bring the mixture to a rolling boil. As soon as the sugar is dissolved, remove the pan from the heat. Let the cordial sit for 30 minutes until it cools to room temperature. (Do not put in the refrigerator to cool.) Use a sieve to strain out the zest, and bottle the liquid. The cordial will keep for 2 to 3 weeks in the refrigerator.

APERITIFS

Many pre-Prohibition cocktails I make at Japp's include an aperitif or fortified wine, such as quinquina and vermouths (sweet and dry). In addition to carrying some of the quality classic vermouth brands, we also make our own vermouth at Japp's. Vermouth is a wine that has been fortified, usually with an unaged brandy, and then aromatized with different herbs, botanicals, and spices. Vermouth has been around since Roman times and was commonly used for medicinal purposes. One of the primary herbs used in making vermouth is wormwood, which is known to help ease digestive problems. The word *vermouth* means wormwood in German. The first commercially produced vermouth was a sweet

vermouth that was made in Italy in the 1700s. A dry vermouth was produced in France soon after. Vermouth is an important ingredient in any classic cocktail that calls for it, especially the martini. In my eyes, it's not a martini unless it has vermouth in it. You'll find vermouth stays fresh and palatable if you store it in the refrigerator rather than on the back of the shelf.

SIMPLE SYRUPS

Simple syrup certainly lives up to its name. It is about the simplest thing to make. It's basically equal parts sugar and water. You can easily flavor it with anything you like simply by adding the flavoring agent to the pot as the sugar is dissolving and then letting it infuse as the syrup cools down.

Bartenders have been using syrup in cocktails for a very long time, and for good reason. Straight sugar takes awhile to dissolve in a drink and mostly lands on the bottom of the glass—causing an unbalanced drink. Adding sugar in syrup form helps the flavor mix quickly and evenly with the other ingredients.

Simple syrup can be made with gum arabic (a natural food stabilizer) to make a silky syrup, and sometimes egg whites are added into simple syrups to help clarify them. But I just use sugar, water, and whatever fresh ingredient I'm flavoring with.

We tend to go through quite a bit of simple syrups at Japp's. Staple flavors we always have on hand are orange, vanilla, ginger,

grenadine, and lavender. I also make a cola syrup and a tonic syrup that will be available for purchase in retail stores. Use the following instructions to create a plain simple syrup. Use these instructions along with the following recipes to create flavored simple syrups.

How to Make Simple Syrup

1. Measure out equal parts water and sugar (1 cup water, 1 cup sugar) in a pot. If creating a flavored syrup, also add the flavoring ingredients to the pot.
2. Bring the mixture to a rolling boil, stirring to prevent scorching.
3. Turn down the heat and let simmer for about 5 minutes.
4. Remove from the heat and let the syrup cool to room temperature.
5. Use a sieve to strain out any solid pieces of spices or flavoring (e.g., vanilla beans) and bottle the syrup. The syrup will keep for 2 to 3 weeks in the refrigerator.

Orange Simple Syrup

1 cup sugar
1 cup water
Zest from 1 orange

Vanilla Simple Syrup

1 cup sugar
1 cup water
2 vanilla beans, split

Ginger Simple Syrup

1 cup sugar

1 cup water

1 cup sliced ginger (you can leave the skin on)

Grenadine Simple Syrup

1 cup sugar

1 cup pomegranate juice

For this recipe, the pomegranate juice replaces the water.

Lavender Simple Syrup

1 cup sugar

1 cup water

1½ cup dried lavender

Spiced Orange Syrup

1 cup sugar

1 cup water

Zest from 2 oranges

1 teaspoon cinnamon

5 cloves

5 whole allspice berries

BITTERS

Bitters are kind of like a spice that gives depth and complexity to a drink. They are an important part of the cocktails we make at Japp's. Bitters are made by infusing herbs (mostly bitter ones) and spices and the dominant flavor ingredient in a high-proof spirit.

The trick is to infuse all the flavors separately and then blend them together to achieve the taste you want.

Many wonderful brands of bitters are on the market today, but two have really stood the test of time: Angostura bitters and Peychaud's Bitters. Bitters were once used as medicine, and both Angostura and Peychaud's have apothecary roots. See the Old Fashion recipe in chapter 5 for the story of Angostura bitters. See the Sazerac recipe in chapter 5 for the story of Peychaud's Bitters.

I say if you enter a bar looking for a cocktail, be sure the establishment uses either Angostura bitters or Peychaud's Bitters. If it doesn't, turn around and walk away, or just get a beer.

At Japp's, we make many different flavors of bitters depending on the cocktail list for the night. I always have Sunshine Bitters in the summer and my homemade tobacco bitters in the colder months. Sunshine Bitters is a recipe I learned from my friend Neya White in San Francisco, and the tobacco bitters is the only secret I keep . . . a girl has to have some kind of mystery!

Sunshine Bitters

This recipe was given to me by my good friend Neya White.

> 1 cup neutral grain spirit (vodka works perfectly)
> ½ ounce crushed cardamom pods
> 1 tablespoon saffron threads
> A mason jar with a lid

Pour the vodka into the mason jar, add the crushed cardamom, and seal the jar with the lid. Store in a room temperature, dark place for about 5 days to let the flavor infuse. Shake daily.

Use a sieve to strain out the cardamom. Add the saffron to the infused vodka. Let the saffron infuse for another day or so. Use a sieve to strain out the saffron, and bottle the liquid.

Orange Bitters

> 1 cup vodka, divided
> Zest from 1 whole orange
> Pith from 1 whole orange
> 2 mason jars with lids

In one mason jar, pour ½ cup of vodka and add the zest. In the other mason jar, add the other ½ cup of vodka and the orange pith. Seal both jars. Store at room temperature in a dark place.

Let the zest and vodka infuse for 1 week. Shake daily. Use a sieve to strain out the zest and return to the jar.

Let the pith and vodka infuse for 10 days. Shake daily. Use a sieve to strain out the pith. Combine both infusions in one bottle.

Cinnamon Bitters

    2 cups vodka, divided
    1 vanilla bean, split
    6 medium-sized cinnamon sticks
    2 mason jars with lids

In one mason jar, add ½ cup of the vodka and the vanilla bean. In the other mason jar, add the remaining 1½ cups of vodka and the cinnamon. Store at room temperature in a dark place.

Let the vanilla bean and vodka infuse for 1 day. Use a sieve to strain out the vanilla bean, and return the liquid to the jar.

Let the cinnamon and vodka infuse for 4 days. Shake daily. Use a sieve to strain out the cinnamon. Combine the two infusions in one bottle.

Allspice Bitters

    1 cup whiskey, divided
    1 vanilla bean, split
    12 allspice berries
    1 tablespoon wormwood
    2 mason jars with lids

In one jar, pour ½ cup of whiskey and the wormwood. In the other jar, add the other ½ cup of whiskey, vanilla bean, and allspice berries. Seal both jars. Store at room temperature in a dark place.

Let the vanilla, allspice, and whiskey infuse for 3 days, and the wormwood and whiskey infuse for 7 days. Shake daily. Use a sieve to strain out the solids and blend to taste in a single jar. Bottle.

3

DRINKS FOR THE MORNING

DRINKING IN THE MORNING was common before Prohibition. In those days, it was often safer to drink liquor than it was to drink water. (I'm also sure it helped to have a nip in the morning after a night of drinking.) While today most people start themselves up with a cup of coffee, back in the day a shot of something strong worked just as well and was just as acceptable.

My great-grandfather Walter C. Hughes drank a shot of whiskey every single morning until he died at age 90. The son of Irish immigrants, Walter was born in Cincinnati in the 1880s. When he was a boy, Walter's father and uncles would send him down to the corner bar to buy a bucket of beer and a newspaper on most days. Walter was the only one who knew how to read, so he would read the paper aloud as the men enjoyed their beer. Sometimes Walter would make up an outrageous story, pretending to read it from the paper, just to watch the men get all riled up! When he was a teen he worked for an ice truck—until he accidentally scared the horse, causing the cart to go over a cliff. He later married Emma Schmalstig (my great-grandmother), a beautiful American-German gal from the West End. Her father didn't approve because Walter wore a cap instead of a proper hat (such a rebel). Walter and Emma raised three children in a house on Glenway Avenue in Price Hill.

NOGGIN CLEANSER *(Pictured)*

Cardamom is an herb commonly used in Middle Eastern dishes. It's also an ingredient in Turkish and Arabic coffee.

> 2 ounces gin
> ½ ounce lime juice, freshly squeezed
> ½ ounce cardamom simple syrup

Add all the ingredients to a shaker. Add ice and shake. Strain into a cocktail glass.

Cardamom Simple Syrup

> 1 cup sugar
> 1 cup water
> 25 crushed cardamom seeds

Follow the directions for making simple syrup in chapter 2.

* * *

THE BEST HANGOVER DRINK EVER

> 1½ ounces gin
> ½ ounce orange juice
> ¼ ounce triple sec
> Dash of absinthe
> Soda to top

Build in a highball glass and top with soda.

WILLIAM III *(Pictured)*

1½ ounces gin

½ ounce Pimm's No. 1

½ ounce spiced orange simple syrup (see chapter 2)

Put all the ingredients in a mixing glass. Add ice. Shake and strain into a cocktail glass. Garnish with an orange twist.

* * *

VAN VOAST COCKTAIL

1½ ounces gin

¾ ounce maraschino liqueur

½ ounce orange juice

2 dashes Pernod liqueur

1 egg white

Coat the inside of an old fashioned glass with Pernod and set aside. Add the gin, maraschino liqueur, orange juice, and egg white to a mixing glass. Add ice and shake vigorously. Strain into the coated old fashioned glass.

SUNSHINE IN A GLASS *(Pictured)*

This cocktail was inspired by a classic cocktail called an Alfonso. The Alfonso was created in Paris in the 1930s, supposedly for King Alfonso XIII of Spain. It's one of the cocktails listed in the famous *Savoy Cocktail Book*. It uses Dubonnet, a fortified wine flavored with a blend of herbs, spices, citrus peel, and quinine. Dubonnet was created to make the harsh taste of quinine easier for the French Foreign legion soldiers to drink during their tours of duty in North Africa.

At the time I came up with Sunshine in a Glass, I couldn't serve Dubonnet in Ohio, so I developed a blond version by using Lillet instead of Dubonnet. Lillet is another French aperitif that has been around since 1872. It is a fortified wine mostly made up of Bordeaux wines and aromatized with sweet and bitter orange peels and quinine. This mixture is then matured in oak casks. It's light enough to let the Sunshine Bitters shine through.

The recipe for the Sunshine Bitters came from my good friend and mentor, Neya White, from San Francisco.

2 ounces Lillet
1 sugar cube
4 dashes Sunshine Bitters (see chapter 2).
Sparkling champagne to top

Place the sugar cube and bitters in a mixing glass and muddle to a paste. Add the Lillet and ice and shake. Strain into a champagne flute and top with champagne. Garnish with a lemon twist.

PRETTY IN PINK MIMOSA

3 ounces fresh ruby red grapefruit juice
½ ounce vanilla simple syrup (see chapter 2)
Champagne to top

Add the grapefruit juice and vanilla simple syrup to a mixing glass. Add ice and stir to chill. Strain into a champagne flute. Top with champagne.

* * *

SPRING IN A GLASS *(Pictured)*

1½ ounces vodka
½ ounce lime juice, freshly squeezed
½ ounce lavender simple syrup (see chapter 2)
3 lychee fruits

Muddle the lychees in a mixing glass. Add vodka, lime juice, and lavender simple syrup. Add ice and shake. Strain into a champagne flute. Garnish with a lime twist.

SUMMER BREEZE *(Pictured)*

> 1½ ounces vodka
> 1 ounce grapefruit juice
> ¾ ounce vanilla simple syrup (see chapter 2)
> 6 mint leaves
> Soda to top

Put all the ingredients except the soda in a mixing glass. Shake and strain into a highball glass filled with ice. Top with soda. Garnish with a sprig of mint.

UNDER THE SEA BLOODY MARY

1½ ounces vodka
1 bar spoon cocktail sauce
½ ounce lemon juice, freshly squeezed
Zing Zang Bloody Mary Mix

Add all the ingredients to a mixing glass. Add ice and shake twice to mix. Pour into a tall glass. Garnish with capers, a cocktail shrimp, and a sprig of dill.

* * *

THE HOBO BLOODY MARY

1½ ounces bourbon
1 bar spoon barbecue sauce
Zing Zang Bloody Mary Mix
Dash of hickory seasoning

Add the bourbon, barbecue sauce, bloody mary mix, and hickory seasoning to a mixing glass. Add ice and shake twice to mix. Pour into a tall glass.

To garnish, skewer 1 piece of beef jerky, 1 cheese cube, and 1 piece of cooked bacon on a toothpick. I also garnish with a few pinto beans and Cheetos.

ST. MARY'S BELL-RINGER

A bell-ringer is cocktail that is usually made up of a spirit, a liqueur or syrup, and bitters, and then poured into a cocktail glass rinsed with apricot brandy. James Maloney created the bell-ringer in the 1890s in Chicago. He had a fondness for apricot brandy and found a way to incorporate it in his drinks whenever possible. This is the bell-ringer I make.

2½ ounces Bulleit bourbon
½ ounce Dolin dry vermouth
2 dashes apricot brandy
Dash of aromatic bitters

Coat a cocktail glass with the apricot brandy and set aside. In a mixing glass add the bourbon, vermouth, and bitters. Add ice, stir, and strain into the coated glass.

PARIS KENTUCKY *(Pictured)*

  1½ ounces bourbon
  ½ ounce apricot simple syrup
  Dash lemon juice, freshly squeezed
  Sparkling champagne to top

Pour the bourbon, apricot simple syrup, and lemon juice into a mixing glass. Add ice and shake. Strain into a champagne flute. Top off with champagne. Garnish with a lemon twist.

Apricot Simple Syrup

  1 cup sugar
  1 cup water
  ½ cup dried apricots

Follow the directions for making simple syrup in chapter 2.

SEELBACH COCKTAIL

The Seelbach was first crafted in 1917 and is named for the famous Seelbach Hotel in Louisville, Kentucky. (It also happens to be Cincinnati Councilman Chris Seelbach's favorite when he comes into Japp's for a drink.) The recipe was lost during Prohibition and rediscovered in 1995 during renovations to the hotel.

This is a great drink to tighten up bourbon. I like to drink these for brunch, but then again, I'm a little freaky. I'm particular about my bourbon anytime, anywhere.

The Seelbach Hotel, Louisville, Kentucky, circa 1900

1½ ounces Bourbon
1 sugar cube
5 dashes Peychaud's Bitters
5 dashes Angostura bitters
½ ounce triple sec
Champagne to top

Add the sugar cube and bitters to a mixing glass and muddle. Add the bourbon, triple sec, and ice to the glass and stir. Strain into a champagne flute and top with champagne.

* * *

GREEN LANTERN

2 ounces tequila
¾ ounce pineapple juice
Fresh cilantro
Fresh mint
1 teaspoon chopped jalapeño

In a mixing glass, muddle the mint, cilantro, jalapeño and pineapple juice. Add the tequila and ice. Shake and double strain into a cocktail glass.

4

DRINKS FOR THE AFTERNOON

DRINKING IN THE AFTERNOON was widely accepted in the 1940s, 50s, and 60s, when the three-martini lunch and a private bar in your office were common practices. My guess is the drinks helped get the creative juices going, or maybe loosened up clients so they could make business decisions easier. But in the 1970s drinking during work was frowned upon, mostly because the bar tabs were written off as business expenses.

I don't think having a tipple during the day is a bad thing, as long as you do it responsibly. Today, a three-martini lunch would put a lot of people under the table, so how did they manage it back then? The secret was moderation—which was enforced by serving sizes. If you look at glassware that was used back in the day, you'll notice it is much smaller than the gigantic monstrosities we see today. The serving size of three martinis back in 1950 would be equivalent to one martini today.

In my line of work, I know it's my job to enjoy liquor and I do. A small drink in the afternoon always gets my creative juices going and it takes the edge off when dealing with so many things all at once, but I'm responsible about it and know that a drink in the afternoon isn't the same as a drink in the evening during a party or a night out.

PORCH SWING *(Pictured)*

2 ounces bourbon
½ ounce raspberry simple syrup
Dash rose water
Sweet tea to top

Build over ice in a highball glass. Top off with sweet tea. Garnish with raspberries and a sprig of mint.

Raspberry Simple Syrup

1 cup sugar
1 cup water
1 cup fresh or frozen raspberries

Follow the directions for making simple syrup in chapter 2.

MINT JULEP

Juleps originated in the Middle East and have been around since 900 A.D. The word *julep* comes from the Arabic word *Julad*, which means rose water. Between the tenth and eighteenth centuries, juleps were made with flowers and herbs, sometimes wormwood and sometimes opium. Alcohol was used instead of water.

Juleps were considered medicine in Europe. It wasn't until they arrived in America that people drank them for fun. In 1784, people in the American Colonies were drinking them in the morning. "Coffee?" "No, thank you, I'll just have a julep."

Americans also introduced mint to juleps. Before the Civil War, mint juleps were the second most popular drink in the United States (behind the sherry cobbler). At this time, juleps were typically made with rum or brandy, Madeira, gin, or applejack if you were in New Jersey.

Bourbon juleps came into fashion after the Civil War. (Though I'm sure if you were in Kentucky before the Civil War, you were most certainly drinking your julep with bourbon.)

Juleps are often associated with horse racing and became the official cocktail of the Kentucky Derby in 1938. Back then you could buy one for seventy-five cents.

While touring the Kentucky Bourbon Trail, I heard a theory as to why horse racing became so popular in Kentucky: Distillers transported their whiskey to New Orleans by shipping it down the Ohio and Mississippi rivers. They would sail their boats down to New Orleans and then buy the fastest horses in town to get back home to Kentucky. Consequently, more and more fast horses ended up in the state. Men soon began bragging about having the

fastest horse, and once the bragging started, the betting and the racing followed close behind. I don't know if that's how it really happened, but it makes sense, and it's a good story, so I'm sticking with it.

The most important thing to remember when making a mint julep is to always use a ton of shaved or crushed ice, and *don't* bruise the mint or it will become bitter. Always garnish with a large, fresh sprig of mint and cut the drinking straw so your nose gets right in the mint while you are drinking. Sip slowly!

 3 ounces bourbon
 ½ ounce mint simple syrup
 1 large mint sprig
 1 ounce dark rum

Pack a julep cup or highball glass with as much crushed ice as possible. In a separate glass, stir together the bourbon and mint syrup. Make a hole in the ice and pour the bourbon mixture in. Top off with the rum and garnish with the mint sprig. Serve with a drinking straw.

Mint Simple Syrup

 1 cup sugar
 1 cup water
 Handful of mint leaves

Follow the directions for making simple syrup in chapter 2.

FIG JIG *(Pictured)*

> 2 ounces bourbon
> 1 ounce Pimm's No. 1
> ½ ounce fig simple syrup

Add all the ingredients in a mixing glass. Add ice and shake. Strain into a cocktail glass.

Fig Simple Syrup

> 1 cup sugar
> 1 cup water
> 6 dried figs cut in half

Follow the directions for making simple syrup in chapter 2.

SMOKED PIMM'S CUP *(Pictured)*

Oysters and gin were London delicacies in the early 1800s. In 1823, James Pimm, proprietor of the Oyster Bar (located in central London), developed a gin sling by flavoring gin with liqueur, fruit, and spices. He called it the "house cup." Pimm went on to create successful scotch and brandy drinks, which became known as house cup No. 2 and house cup No. 3, respectively. The gin sling remained house cup No. 1. When Pimm began commercially bottling his gin-based liqueur, he stuck with his original naming scheme, and the drink was sold as Pimm's No. 1.

> 2 ounces Pimm's No. 1
> ¾ ounces smoked ginger simple syrup
> Soda to top

Build in a old fashioned glass over ice and top with soda. Garnish with a slice of ginger, a wedge of lemon, and a cucumber slice.

Smoked Ginger Simple Syrup

> 1 cup sugar
> 1 cup water
> 1 small handful of ginger, sliced
> ½ teaspoon hickory powder

Follow the directions for making simple syrup in chapter 2.

SCARLETT O'HARA

The Scarlett O'Hara is one of the earliest Southern Comfort cocktails. It was made to commemorate the movie *Gone With the Wind* in 1939.

Southern Comfort was invented in 1874 in New Orleans by a bartender named Martin W. Heron. Back in those days, lots of whiskey was being shipped down the Mississippi River to New Orleans. Not all of it was quality stuff, and the taste was always different, never consistent. So in order to serve a consistent and quality product, Heron came up with a recipe using nuts and spices that were readily available in the thriving port of New Orleans. He eventually came up with a fantastic whiskey liqueur he originally named "Cuffs and Buttons." That name was chosen to compete with another popular liqueur of the day, "Hats and Tails."

Just inside the gates of the St. Louis World's Fair, circa 1904.

Heron, who was originally from St. Louis, brought his product to the 1904 World's Fair and won first place for taste and quality.

1½ ounces Southern Comfort
1 ounce cranberry juice
½ ounce lime juice, freshly squeezed

Add all the ingredients to a mixing glass. Add ice and shake. Strain into a cocktail glass.

PISCO PUNCH

This recipe uses pineapple gum syrup. Find it at a local specialty foods store or purchase it online from at smallhandfoods.com.

> 2 ounces pisco brandy
> ½ ounce lemon juice, freshly squeezed
> ½ ounce pineapple gum syrup

Add all the ingredients to a mixing glass. Add ice and shake. Strain into a cocktail glass.

* * *

KNICKERBOCKER

> 1½ ounces rum
> ¾ ounce lime juice, freshly squeezed
> ½ ounce raspberry simple syrup (see the Porch Swing recipe)
> ¼ ounce triple sec

Build the drink in a cocktail glass filled with shaved ice. Garnish with a raspberry.

SHERRY COBBLER

The sherry cobbler was the most popular drink in the United States in the mid to late 1800s. It's a true American drink. The first mention of the drink was in *How to Mix Drinks: The Bon-Vivant's Companion*, written in 1862 by Jerry Thomas.

Sherry is a fortified wine made in Spain. It is produced from white grapes and fortified with brandy. The flavor of sherry ranges from dry to bold or sweet to jammy.

Cobbler can be used to describe many things, from a shoemaker to dessert, but when used in the context

Sherry comes from the Jerez region in the south of Spain.

of a mixed drink, a cobbler is defined as spirit, sugar, fruit, and crushed ice topped with fruit and served with a drinking straw. The best way to make the original version of this drink is to muddle the ice and the orange together.

The mix of sherry with a muddled orange and sugar, and topped with berries, seems perfect for summer. The original recipe called for a muddled orange, but you can experiment with any fresh fruit or spirit. The most important parts of the drink are the crushed ice and the drinking straw.

1½ ounces sherry
½ ounce triple sec
1 slice fresh orange
1 bar spoon of blueberries
1 strawberry (chopped)
Soda to top

In a highball glass, add the orange slice and sherry and give it a slight muddle. Add the triple sec. Fill the glass three-fourths with crushed ice. Place the blueberries and strawberry on top of the ice and top off with soda. Garnish with a mint sprig and an orange slice. Serve with a drinking straw.

KITTY BURKE *(Pictured)*

The Kitty Burke was inspired by a Cincinnati burlesque dancer. Kitty was one of the most popular ladies of the burlesque scene in the 1930s.

She loved baseball and especially loved to watch the Red Stockings play at Crosley Field. At a sold-out night game in July 1935, Kitty heckled the batters all night. She finally got fed up and walked onto the field and over to home plate, where she took the bat from Reds player Babe Herman to show him how to hit. St. Louis Cardinals pitcher Paul "Daffy" Dean threw her a pitch, which she hit. The hit didn't count because Kitty wasn't on the roster (a minor detail), but the incident put her on the map as the first woman to hit a baseball in a major league game.

Kitty's baseball escapade increased her fame. The Reds gave her an official uniform that she used in her burlesque acts (which may be the best use of a Reds uniform on or off the field).

I make this drink with a little orange blossom water for a feminine touch. It's the perfect drink for bad-ass women to drink while watching and playing baseball better than men! Amen, sister!

Kitty Burke at bat.

2 ounces gin

2 bar spoons triple sec

1 bar spoon orange blossom water

2 cucumber wheels

6 mint leaves

Soda to top

continued

In a mixing glass, muddle all the mint and cucumber. Add the gin, triple sec, and orange blossom water. Add ice and shake. Strain over ice into an old fashioned glass. Top with soda. Garnish with a sprig of mint and a cucumber wheel.

* * *

LAST WORD

This cocktail was developed at the Detroit Athletic Club during the 1920s. It was introduced by vaudeville entertainer Frank Fogarty, who was one of the best monologists in the early twentieth century. The Detroit Athletic Club is a private social club founded in 1887. It was formed for the betterment of athletes and started out basically as a huge field. A clubhouse was built to prevent a road from being built through the field. It was a place where athletes could train and relax.

The Athletic Club used bathtub gin during Prohibition, and the Last Word was a great cocktail that disguised the harsh flavor. It shows up in Ted Saucier's 1951 cocktail book, *Bottoms Up*.

1½ ounces gin
½ ounce lime juice, freshly squeezed
½ ounce maraschino liqueur
¼ ounce chartreuse

Add all the ingredients in a mixing glass. Add ice, shake, and strain into a cocktail glass.

SINGAPORE SLING

The Singapore Sling was created by Ngiam Tong Boon at the Long Bar in the Raffles Hotel in Singapore around 1915. Raffles Hotel is, and was, considered a grand hotel that dates back to 1887. It was very popular with British and American visitors.

The cocktail started out as a drink called Straits Sling before Boon brought it with him to the Long Bar. In addition to the name change, this cocktail has undergone some other changes. The version served today at the Long Bar was developed by Boon's nephew, who worked at the bar in the 1970s.

The word *sling* comes from a German word that means to swallow or drink. Originally slings were made from a spirit, bitters, citrus, carbonated water, sugar, and ice. Some people preferred a sprinkle of grated nutmeg on top to finish it off. Slings were a popular summer drink in the 1800s. Hot climates like Singapore demanded a refreshing drink, and its namesake Sling filled the bill.

   1½ ounces gin
   ½ ounce Heering Cherry Liqueur
   ½ ounce Bénédictine
   1 dash lime juice, freshly squeezed
   Soda to top

Add the gin, Heering, Bénédictine, and lime juice to a highball glass. Add ice and top off with soda.

MARY B *(Pictured)*

2 ounces gin

¼ of a kiwi, peeled and chopped

2 dashes absinthe

Tonic water to top

In a shaker, muddle the kiwi. Add gin, absinthe, ice, and shake. Strain into an old fashioned glass filled with ice. Top with tonic water and garnish with slices of kiwi.

* * *

TOM COLLINS

1½ ounces gin

½ ounce lemon juice, freshly squeezed

½ ounce triple sec

Soda to top

Build in a highball glass full of ice and top with soda.

KOALA COCKTAIL *(Pictured)*

2 ounces gin
½ ounce lemon juice, freshly squeezed
½ ounce eucalyptus simple syrup
1 green apple wedge

In a shaker, muddle the apple. Add the gin, lemon juice, syrup, and ice. Shake and strain into a cocktail glass. Garnish with an apple slice.

Eucalyptus Simple Syrup

1 cup sugar
1 cup water
½ cup dried eucalyptus

Follow the directions for making simple syrup in chapter 2.

CHILL OUT BARBRA *(Pictured)*

    1½ ounces gin
    ½ ounce lime juice, freshly squeezed
    1 bar spoon rhubarb jam
    Soda to top

Put all ingredients, except soda, in a shaker. Add ice and shake well. Strain into an ice-filled highball glass and top with soda. Garnish with a lime twist.

THE BEE'S KNEES

The expression *bee's knees* came about in the 1920s. It's a slang term that means the height of excellence or the cream of the crop. No one is completely certain where this saying came from. One theory is that it's from the B's and the E's in another popular phrase, *be-all and end-all.*

Another theory is that the phrase refers to a popular dancer of the day, Bee Jackson. Bee was a champion Charleston dancer who danced all over the world.

Flappers dance the Charleston near the U.S. Capitol, circa 1920.

She didn't invent the Charleston, but no one danced it better than Bee. She was quite a character, and once punched the king of Albania in the nose. (I'm sure Bee had a very good reason.) She died at the age of twenty-five of a ruptured appendix.

Back to the cocktail. The Bee's Knees is a Prohibition drink. It was created to help mask the taste of the bathtub gin. The recipe was first seen in print in the 1930s. After drinking a few of these, you'll be kicking up your heels just like Bee Jackson.

1½ ounces gin
½ ounce honey simple syrup
½ ounce lemon juice, freshly squeezed

Add all the ingredients to a mixing glass. Add ice, shake, and strain into a cocktail glass. Garnish with a lemon twist.

Honey Simple Syrup

   1 cup water
   1 cup honey

Combine the water and the honey in a pan over medium heat. Stir continually until the honey and water are evenly combined.

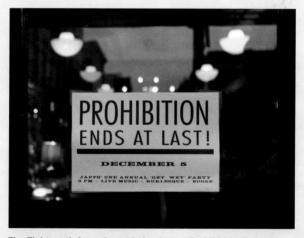

The Eighteenth Amendment helped start Prohibition, but it was repealed by the Twenty-first Amendment in 1933. At Japp's we throw a repeal day party every December to commemorate the return of legal liquor.

CHERRY BOMB *(Pictured)*

At Japp's, we use a juicer to make our own fresh fennel juice. Cut a fresh fennel bulb to fit the opening of your juicer and juice. It will keep for four days in the refrigerator.

> 1½ ounces gin
> ½ ounce fennel juice
> ½ ounce vanilla simple syrup (see chapter 2 for recipe)
> ¼ ounce lemon juice, freshly squeezed
> 5 bing cherries

Add the cherries to a mixing glass. Muddle and add the rest of the ingredients. Add ice and shake. Double strain into a cocktail glass. Garnish with a cherry.

AM I BLUE *(Pictured)*

   1½ ounces gin
   ½ ounce blueberry simple syrup
   ½ ounce lime juice, freshly squeezed
   Fresh basil
   Soda to top

Muddle the basil with the blueberry syrup in a mixing glass. Add the gin, lime juice, and ice. Shake. Double strain into a highball glass over ice. Top off with soda. Garnish with blueberries and a sprig of fresh basil.

Blueberry Simple Syrup

   1 cup sugar
   1 cup water
   ½ cup fresh or frozen blueberries

Follow the directions for making simple syrup in chapter 2.

CALM DOWN *(Pictured)*

　　1½ ounces gin
　　½ ounce lemon juice, freshly squeezed
　　½ ounce chamomile simple syrup

Add all the ingredients to a mixing glass. Add ice and shake. Strain into a cocktail glass.

Chamomile Simple Syrup

　　1 cup sugar
　　1 cup water
　　½ cup dried chamomile flowers

Follow the directions for making simple syrup in chapter 2.

FLIPS

A flip is a type of cocktail that is identified by a light, fluffy texture. Flips date back to the 1600s, when they were made by mixing beer, rum, and sugar and heating the drink with a red-hot iron called a loggerhead. The loggerhead would warm the drink and cause the beer to froth. The frothing was *flipping* the drink. Over time, egg whites were used to froth the drink instead of beer. The egg whites make the texture light and fluffy. No slime. Think of the meringue on pie.

Yes, the egg whites are raw, but please don't freak out. Of course, salmonella is no joking matter, but according to the National Safety Council, you're more likely to choke on a handful of bar nuts than you are to get salmonella poisoning from one of these drinks.

* * *

BUMBLE BEE COCKTAIL

2 ounces dark rum
½ ounce honey
½ ounce lime juice, freshly squeezed
1 egg white

Add all ingredients to a mixing glass. Fill with ice and shake vigorously. Strain into a cocktail glass. Garnish with a lime twist.

AMARETTO SOUR

    2 ounces amaretto
    ½ ounce lemon juice, freshly squeezed
    1 egg white

Add all the ingredients to a mixing glass. Add ice, shake vigorously, and strain into a cocktail glass.

* * *

PISCO SOUR

    1½ ounces pisco brandy
    ½ ounce lemon juice, freshly squeezed
    ½ ounce triple sec
    1 egg white
    1 dash of Angostura bitters

Add all the ingredients, except the bitters, to a mixing glass. Add ice and shake vigorously. Strain into a small rocks glass. Top with a dash of bitters.

ROSY CHEEKS *(Pictured)*

> 1½ ounces gin
> ½ ounce spiced cranberry simple syrup
> 1 egg white
> Juice of half of a fresh lime

Put all the ingredients in a mixing glass. Add ice and shake vigorously. Strain into a cocktail glass.

Spiced Cranberry Simple Syrup

> 1 cup sugar
> 1 cup cranberry juice
> 1 teaspoon cinnamon
> 5 whole cloves
> 5 allspice berries

Follow the directions for making simple syrup in chapter 2.

CLOVER CLUB

The Clover Club cocktail was created before Prohibition. Its name comes from the Philadelphia Clover Club Men's Club, which met at the Bellevue-Stratford Hotel. It was the hotel's signature drink. The combination of these ingredients will surprise you, especially if you are normally not a huge fan of gin. All the flavors in this drink mingle together like magic and cover up the harsh parts of the gin.

  1 ounce gin
  ½ ounce lemon juice, freshly squeezed
  ½ ounce grenadine
  1 egg white

Add all the ingredients to a mixing glass. Add ice and shake vigorously. Strain into a cocktail glass.

* * *

ELKS CLUB FIZZ

  1½ ounces whiskey
  1 ounce port
  ½ ounce lemon juice, freshly squeezed
  ½ ounce triple sec
  1 egg white

Add all the ingredients to a mixing glass. Add ice and shake vigorously. Strain into a cocktail glass. Garnish with pineapple chunks.

RAMOS GIN FIZZ

This is one of New Orleans' most famous drinks. It was invented in 1888 by Henry C. Ramos, or Henrico Ramos, at the Imperial Cabinet Saloon in New Orleans. Back in those days, it was not unusual to have a dozen or more bartenders working together behind the bar.

The trick to making a perfect Ramos Gin Fizz is to shake the holy you-know-what out of it until all the ice is gone. The drink is supposed to be shaken for ten minutes. So in Henry's day, the bartenders would continuously pass the shakers down the row, each taking a turn shaking. It must have been quite a sight. During Mardi Gras in 1915, Ramos had thirty-five shaker boys behind the bar shaking their arms off.

This drink is like a dream. The most interesting thing about it is the mix of orange blossom water and egg white. The prolonged shaking makes the drink silky and totally integrates the cream and the egg whites with the complexity of the sweet, sour, and floral flavors. It's wonderful.

1½ ounces gin (Old Tom, if you have it)
½ ounce triple sec
½ ounce lemon juice, freshly squeezed
½ ounce heavy cream
1 egg white
1 dash of orange blossom water

Add all the ingredients to a mixing glass. Add ice and shake for—like—*ever* (until the ice is gone)! Strain into a highball glass and garnish with a lemon twist.

PEAR-SHAPED DIAMOND *(Pictured)*

> 1½ ounces vodka
> ¾ ounce vanilla simple syrup (see chapter 2 for recipe)
> ¼ ounce fresh pear juice
> Dash of cinnamon bitters (see chapter 2 for recipe)

Add all the ingredients to a mixing glass. Add ice. Shake and strain into a cocktail glass. Garnish with a mini-pear if you wish.

5

HAPPY HOUR DRINKS

HAPPY HOUR IS THE PERFECT WAY to help shake off the day. It's a time to unwind and socialize and remind yourself that you work to live, not live to work.

The name *happy hour* originated in the 1920s. It was a slang term used by sailors in the Navy to refer to the time set aside for on-ship entertainment. During Prohibition, speakeasies applied the slang to the hour when patrons would come in for an aperitif before dinner.

Having a cocktail is a great way to begin dinner for a few reasons. It gives you time to slow down from your day and separate the stress of work from the enjoyment of your personal life. You'll be relaxed when you sit down to eat so you'll enjoy your meal more. Certain cocktails can also help build your appetite and help ready your stomach to receive a meal. They are known as aperitifs. Again, the key to drinking during the day is moderation. There's no need to go overboard. One or two cocktails before dinner will put you in the perfect mood for a very enjoyable meal.

MOSCOW MULE

To understand the origins of the Moscow Mule, you have to know a little about the history of vodka in America. Before the 1940s, unless you were Russian or Eastern European, you did not drink vodka. No one liked the stuff! Rudolph Kunett, a Russian-American, was bound and determined to convince Americans otherwise.

With the best of intentions and the highest of hopes, Kunett purchased the rights to produce Smirnoff vodka in the United States. His enthusiasm was met with total indifference from the masses. Americans loved their gin, whiskey, and brandy, but no one was interested in adding vodka to their list of favorite spirits. Kunett was broke. He sold the Smirnoff rights to John Martin for the price of the distilling equipment. If only Kunett had known what the future held.

John Martin teamed up with Jack Morgan, owner of the Cock 'n Bull restaurant on the Sunset Strip in Hollywood. Morgan had an overstock of ginger beer and a friend in the copper business who was happy to supply him with copper mugs. Put all those elements together—vodka, ginger beer, and a copper mug—and you have a magical cocktail, the Moscow Mule.

Martin knew the cocktail could be key to improving the sales of vodka, but he had to come up with a way to persuade other Hollywood bartenders to make the drink for their customers. Morgan decided to ask area bartenders to make the Moscow Mule and then have their pictures taken with the drink. Morgan went bar to bar showing the photos and persuading bartenders to follow suit. Little by little, the cocktail became *the* drink of the Hollywood elite. In the 1950s anybody who was anybody was drinking a Moscow

Mule with plenty of vodka. The original recipe is 1½ ounces vodka, a dash of lime juice, and topped with ginger beer. This is how we make the Moscow Mule at Japp's.

1½ ounces vodka
½ ounce ginger simple syrup (see chapter 2 for recipe)
Dash of lime juice, freshly squeezed
Soda to top

Add the vodka, lime juice, and ginger syrup to a highball glass. Add ice and top with soda.

* * *

MIKE ROMANOFF COCKTAIL

Mike Romanoff was a dapper and charming Hollywood figure in the 1950s. He was born Hershel Geguzin in Lithuania in the 1890s and grew up in orphanages. At age ten, he immigrated alone to the United States, where he once again spent time in orphanages and reform schools.

In America, he changed his name to Harry Gerguson, but after moving to Hollywood in the 1930s, he reinvented himself and started going by the name Prince Michael Dimitri Alexandrovich Obolensky-Romanoff and pretended to be the nephew of Tsar Nicholas II of Russia. The story was known to be false, but it fit with the attitude of the town, so everyone went along with the ruse. Romanoff made many friends in Hollywood, including Humphrey Bogart and David Niven, who were among his best friends.

He started Romanoffs in Beverly Hills, and it turned out to be one of the most popular restaurants in town, hosting the elite

of Hollywood in the 1950s. The Romanoff cocktail was created at Romanoffs in 1955 and named, of course, for the suave imposter. It is one of the rare early vodka cocktails.

> 1½ ounces vodka
> ¼ ounce triple sec
> ½ ounce apricot liqueur
> ¼ ounce lime juice, freshly squeezed
> Dash of bitters

Add all the ingredients to a mixing glass. Add ice, shake, and strain into a cocktail glass.

* * *

SPICY MAN *(Pictured)*

> 2 ounces vodka
> ½ ounce five-spice simple syrup
> 6 mandarin orange slices
> Soda to top

Add the mandarin oranges to a mixing glass and muddle. Add the vodka, five-spice syrup, ice, and shake. Strain into a highball glass full of ice. Top with soda. Garnish with a mandarin orange slice.

Five-Spice Simple Syrup

> 1 cup sugar
> 1 cup water
> 1 teaspoon five-spice powder

Follow the directions for making simple syrup in chapter 2.

SWEETE HEAT *(Pictured)*

> 2 ounces vodka
> 2 bar spoons jalapeño simple syrup
> Dash of salt and pepper

Add the vodka and jalapeño syrup to a mixing glass. Add ice and shake. Strain into a cocktail glass. Add a dash of salt and pepper. Garnish with a jalapeño slice.

Jalapeño Simple Syrup

> 1 cup sugar
> 1 cup water
> 1 chopped jalapeño

Follow the directions for making simple syrup in chapter 2.

ROSEMARY'S SECRET *(Pictured)*

  2 ounces vodka
  1 ounce grapefruit juice, freshly squeezed
  ½ ounce Rosemary simple syrup

Add all the ingredients to a mixing glass. Add ice and shake. Strain into a cocktail glass. Garnish with a sprig of rosemary.

Rosemary Simple Syrup

  1 cup sugar
  1 cup water
  4 sprigs rosemary

Follow the directions for making simple syrup in chapter 2.

CILANTRO BLOSSOM *(Pictured)*

> 1½ ounces vodka
> ½ ounce ginger syrup (see chapter 2 for recipe)
> ½ ounce lemon juice, freshly squeezed
> Dash of orange blossom water
> 12 cilantro leaves
> Soda to top

Add the cilantro and orange blossom water to a mixing glass and muddle. Add the rest of the ingredients. Fill with ice and shake. Double strain into an old fashioned glass filled with ice. Top off with soda. Garnish with cilantro leaves and a lemon twist.

GREEN MONSTER *(Pictured)*

In this recipe, the brand of vodka matters. Bison Grass Vodka infused with Hierochloe odorata. This herb is more commonly known as sweetgrass, holy grass, and (in Eastern Europe) buffalo grass. The Polish infuse vodka with buffalo grass and call the resulting drink Żubrówka.

> 1½ ounces Bison Grass Vodka
> ½ of a lime
> 6 green grapes
> Dash of chartreuse to coat glass

Coat a cocktail glass with chartreuse and set aside. In a mixing glass, muddle six grapes and half a lime. Add vodka and ice and shake. Double strain into the chartreuse-coated cocktail glass. Garnish with a green grape.

OLD FASHION

Angostura bitters was developed in 1824 by a German surgeon, Dr. Johann G.B. Siegert, who served as surgeon general for the Venezuelan army. While stationed in the port town of Angostura (now called Ciudad Bolívar or Bolivar City), Siegert spent four years developing the formula for a tonic to help soldiers with stomach ailments and sailors with seasickness. He named the tonic after the town. The bitters caught on, and Siegert opened a distillery in 1830. After the good surgeon passed away in 1875, his son moved the distillery to Port of Spain, Trinidad. The bitters are still sold today in bottles with labels that are too large for them. According to the company, the labels don't match the bottles because one of Siegert's sons was in charge of labels and the other was in charge of bottles. There was a miscommunication between the two brothers, causing the error that has now become a trademark.

> 2 ounces rye
> 1 sugar cube
> 2 dashes Angostura bitters

Add the sugar cube and bitters to a rocks glass and muddle. Add the rye and ice. Stir. Garnish with a lemon peel.

MANHATTAN *(Pictured)*

The manhattan was introduced in the early 1870s at the Manhattan Club. The Madison Avenue mansion housed a six-hundred seat theater and a breakfast room that could seat seventy people. That's a lot of bacon and eggs! During this era, clubs became famous for their unique cocktails. People ordered a drink by the name of the club in which they first had the drink. Thus the manhattan was born.

As a side note, the Manhattan Club was once owned by the very wealthy Jerome family. In the mid to late nineteenth century, wealthy American families sent their older daughters, along with a chaperone, to Europe for several months to do the "tour." On the surface, this trip was to introduce the women to European culture. The real purpose was to introduce the eligible young ladies

A view of the New York City skyline from the Manhattan Bridge, circa 1910.

to eligible young royalty with the hopes of landing a rich husband, a title, a castle, and lots and lots of money. It worked in the case of the Jerome family. While on her European tour, Jennie Jerome met and married Lord Randolph Churchill. Their son was Winston Churchill.

The manhattan is a drink that has stood the test of time and rolled with the changing tastes of society. It is still a very popular cocktail. During Prohibition, people developed a taste for Canadian whisky in their manhattans, and then changed to bourbon when Prohibition ended. Any whiskey will do just fine.

I prefer to use rye rather than bourbon in this cocktail. Rye was the whiskey of choice by the late 1800s. I love the spicy kick the rye gives the drink. It holds up against the vermouth and plays with the bitters.

2 ounces rye
½ ounce sweet vermouth
2 dashes bitters

Combine all the ingredients in a mixing glass, add ice, and stir until well chilled. Strain into a chilled cocktail glass. Garnish with a cherry.

ALGONQUIN COCKTAIL

The algonquin cocktail was quite popular in the 1920s. It was named for the Algonquin Hotel, where a group of writers, actors, and some of the wittiest people in show business would regularly banter around the hotel's infamous round table. During their daily "meeting," they exchanged witty stories, anecdotes, and jokes.

On any given day, you might find Dorothy Parker, George S. Kaufman, and Robert Benchley. The Marx Brothers, Alexander Woollcott, and Harold Ross also stopped in now and then to take a seat at the round table. They would all drink something, not necessarily algonquin cocktails, but maybe gin martinis or highballs.

1½ ounces rye
½ ounce French vermouth
½ ounce pineapple juice

Add all the ingredients to a mixing glass. Add ice and shake. Strain into a cocktail glass.

PLUM CRAZY *(Pictured)*

2 ounces bourbon
½ ounce Heering Cherry Liqueur
½ ounce plum juice
½ ounce lemon juice, freshly squeezed

Add all the ingredients to a mixing glass. Add ice and shake. Strain into a cocktail glass. Garnish with a lemon twist.

* * *

BOURBON DAISY

A "daisy" drink is basically a spirit with soda served with cracked or shaved ice. It also will include a sweet part (usually triple sec, grenadine, or gum syrup and later pineapple juice) and a sour element like lemon, lime, or orange juice.

Daisy was Victorian slang for swell or terrific. Daisy drinks were created in the late 1840s to early 1850s, but they really became popular in the 1880s. Most people enjoyed them as refreshing drinks at the end of a hot day because they were always served cold with a lot of ice.

1½ ounces bourbon
½ ounce triple sec
½ ounce lemon juice, freshly squeezed
½ ounce grenadine

Add the bourbon, triple sec, and lemon juice to an old fashioned glass. Add ice and stir. Slowly drizzle grenadine down the side of the glass so it lies on the bottom.

BEES IN KILTS *(Pictured)*

1½ ounces scotch
½ ounce lavender honey
¼ ounce lemon juice, freshly squeezed

Add all the ingredients to a mixing glass. Add ice, shake, and strain into a cocktail glass. Garnish with a lemon twist.

* * *

BLOOD AND SAND

On the surface, Blood and Sand may be one of the least appetizing cocktail names, but it actually takes its name from a fantastic 1922 silent movie starring Rudolph Valentino as a bullfighter. The original recipe calls for the juice of blood oranges, which is red. It appears in the 1930 *Savoy Cocktail Book*.

1½ ounces scotch
1 ounce orange juice, freshly squeezed
½ ounce Heering Cherry Liqueur
½ ounce sweet vermouth

Add all the ingredients to a mixing glass. Add ice and shake vigorously. Strain into a cocktail glass.

MARTINEZ COCKTAIL

The Martinez is the grandfather of the martini, although the only thing the two drinks have in common is the use of gin. It's a fantastic cocktail!

The story goes that this cocktail was created in the 1880s at the Occidental Hotel in San Francisco. It was made for a man traveling to the nearby town of Martinez, which inspired the name. The recipe was first written down by Jerry Thomas.

Thomas is considered the father of mixology, and author of the first cocktail book, *The Bar-Tender's Guide* (also titled *How to Mix Drinks: The Bon-Vivant's Companion*) in 1862. The revised 1887 edition includes a recipe for the Martinez.

The Occidental Hotel, San Francisco, circa 1866

Thomas was from New York and learned to bar tend in Connecticut. From there, he traveled to San Francisco during the Gold Rush. After the rush he returned to New York and opened a saloon. He spent a lot of time traveling the country and even parts of Europe. He carried his own set of solid silver bar tools and earned a reputation for his knowledge of mixology and cocktail recipes. He became quite the celebrity. While working at the Occidental in San Francisco, he earned a salary larger than the vice president of the United States.

Old Tom Gin was very popular in the 1700s and 1800s. It's a lightly sweetened gin. The sweetener was added to cover up the harshness of the gin. Legend has it that Old Tom Gin gets its name from a shop run by Captain Dudley Bradstreet. Bradstreet painted a big black cat on the door. Under the cat's paw was a slot and the end of a pipe that led to a funnel inside the shop. Customers would put money in the slot and get a shot of gin from the pipe. Dudley advertised the availability of gin from under the old tomcat, and what do you know? America's first unofficial vending machine was born!

1½ ounces gin (Old Tom, if you have it)
½ ounce sweet vermouth
½ ounce maraschino liqueur
Dash of orange bitters (see chapter 2 for recipe)

Add all the ingredients to a mixing glass. Add ice and stir. Strain into a cocktail glass and garnish with an orange twist.

CLASSIC MARTINI

The martini evolved from the Martinez, which is made with Old Tom Gin, maraschino, sweet vermouth, and bitters. Over time, the drink was made with just the gin and sweet vermouth, and then the sweet vermouth was switched up for dry vermouth in the 1880s. If you are a serious martini drinker, vermouth should be a staple in your bar. Keep it fresh by storing it in the refrigerator.

The vodka variation of the martini was introduced in the 1940s when vodka makers were desperately trying to sell the liquor to American drinkers. However, gin and vermouth complement each other better than vodka and vermouth. (Even if you are not a big gin drinker, you would be surprised by how many beautiful non-Christmas-tree-tasting gins are on the market today. It's worth giving gin another try!)

A martini is always stirred because you want it to be cold, but also clear and soft. Shaking the drink will make it cloudy and just a bit sharper in the mouth. Some folks like their martinis shaken, but in my book, the shake transforms it from a martini to another cocktail known as a Bradford. Historically, many bartenders would shake martinis (Bradfords) when they were using potato vodka, which tends to be a bit oily compared to the grain vodkas that are much more popular today. Shaking the potato vodka martinis would help distribute the oil more evenly.

Martinis are one of the most classic drinks out there. I drink these often with my family. Everyone has his or her own opinion about what makes a proper martini. In my opinion, a proper martini is made with either gin or vodka. It must contain dry

vermouth, and it is always stirred. It can be served on the rocks or straight up. And it can be garnished with an olive or a twist.

    3 ounces gin or vodka
    2 bar spoons dry vermouth

Add both ingredients to a mixing glass over ice. Stir. Strain into a chilled cocktail glass. Garnish with an olive or a twist.

* * *

VESPER MARTINI

This is a James Bond martini. It first appeared in Ian Fleming's debut James Bond novel, *Casino Royale*. In the book, Bond likes to enjoy one very strong, very large, and very cold cocktail before dinner (the drink also helps him concentrate, apparently). He orders this martini with grain vodka rather than potato vodka and has it shaken, not stirred, so it is very, very cold. (My variation is stirred to keep the drink clear and soft.) Bond names the drink for the novel's lead female character, Vesper.

    1 ounce gin
    1 ounce vodka
    1 ounce Lillet

Add all the ingredients to a mixing glass. Add ice, stir, and strain into a cocktail glass.

FRENCH 75 *(Pictured)*

In 1916, before America entered World War I, a group of thirty-eight American fighter pilots, all volunteers, went to France and joined the Lafayette Escadrille, a small squadron that was part of the French air service.

The American pilots quickly developed a taste for French champagne, but wanted a bit more kick to it, so they added some cognac. They christened their concoction the French 75 after the French 75mm howitzer artillery piece used in the war.

At some point, this drink crossed the channel and became popular in Britain. The Brits, however, added gin instead of cognac. Either addition works well.

The war is long over, the howitzer has ceased fire, but the French 75 remains a popular cocktail. Vive la France!

1½ ounces gin or cognac
1 sugar cube
Dash of lemon juice, freshly squeezed
Champagne to top

In a mixing glass, muddle the sugar cube and lemon juice together. Add gin and ice and shake. Strain into a champagne flute and top off with champagne. Garnish with a lemon twist.

MAIDEN'S PRAYER

The Maiden's Prayer cocktail takes its name from a 1856 song written by Polish composer Tekla Badarzewska-Baranowska. The song was super popular all through Europe and America, and the piano arrangement was the best-selling sheet music in the 1890s. John Stowell Adams, an American writer, wrote English-language lyrics for the song in the 1890s. In the 1930s, American singer Bob Wills created a country-music arrangement of the tune. Now Willie Nelson sings it.

The song was so popular at the turn of the century that a cocktail was named for it in 1907.

1½ ounces gin
½ ounce triple sec
½ ounce orange juice, freshly squeezed
½ ounce lemon juice, freshly squeezed

Add all the ingredients to a mixing glass. Add ice and shake. Strain into a cocktail glass.

AVIATION

The Aviation cocktail was created by barman Hugo Ensslin around 1911. It's included in the 1916 cocktail book he wrote entitled *Recipes for Mixed Drinks*. The Aviation was a popular drink until Prohibition, at which time it became impossible to find crème de violette. In fact, *The Savoy Cocktail Book*, 1930 edition, doesn't even list crème de violette in its Aviation recipe.

The dash of crème de violette gives this drink a soft hint of blue, like the sky, and with the addition of maraschino liqueur, the drink acquires a unique flavor.

Maraschino is a cherry liqueur flavored with marasca cherries, which are grown in northern Italy. The cherries and the pits are distilled like a brandy. After the distilling process is completed, the liqueur is poured into uncharred ashen casks and left to age for two years. The ash wood casks lend no color, just flavor. Once the liqueur has aged sufficiently, it's diluted and sugar is added.

> 1½ ounces gin
> ½ ounce lemon juice, freshly squeezed
> ½ ounce maraschino liqueur
> 2 dashes crème de violette

Add the gin, lemon juice, and maraschino to a mixing glass. Add ice and shake. Strain into a cocktail glass. Drizzle in the crème de violette. Garnish with a lemon twist.

SOUTHSIDE

This is a fantastic cocktail and one I often make to convince people that gin can taste good (especially if you think you hate gin because you've only had gin with tonic from a bar gun).

This cocktail made its start in the speakeasies of Chicago before it managed to make it to the glitzy men's clubs of South Hampton.

During Prohibition, Chicago was divided by gangs that controlled the illegal liquor trade. The Northside gang, run by Al Capone and Johnny Torrio, controlled the high-quality spirits smuggled in from Canada. The Southside, run by the Saltis-McErlane gang, was left to run bathtub gin to their speakeasies. The bathtub gin was horrible, so sugar, lemon, and mint were added to disguise the flavor. The resulting cocktail was called a Southside.

Eventually, it became a popular summertime drink in the Hamptons, where it was served in a highball glass and topped with soda.

1½ ounces gin
½ ounce lemon juice, freshly squeezed
½ ounce triple sec
6 mint leaves

Add all the ingredients to a mixing glass. Fill with ice and shake. Double strain into a cocktail glass. Garnish with additional mint leaves.

COMMUNIST COCKTAIL

    1½ ounces gin

    1 ounce orange juice, freshly squeezed

    ½ ounce Heering Cherry Liqueur

    ½ ounce lemon juice, freshly squeezed

Add all the ingredients to a mixing glass. Add ice and shake vigorously. Strain into a cocktail glass.

* * *

GABY DE LYS

    2 ounces gin

    ½ ounce orgeat syrup

    Dash of absinthe

Coat a cocktail glass with the absinthe. Add the gin, orgeat syrup, and ice to a mixing glass. Shake vigorously. Strain into the coated cocktail glass.

Vintage absinthe fountain

SUDDENLY SEAMORE *(Pictured)*

2 ounces gin
½ ounce St. Germain liqueur
½ ounce lemon juice, freshly squeezed
Dash of Campari liqueur

Add the gin, St. Germain, lemon juice, and ice to a mixing glass and shake. Strain into a cocktail glass. Drizzle Campari down the side of the glass so it rests on the bottom.

* * *

ATTENTION COCKTAIL

1½ ounces gin
½ ounce dry vermouth
¼ ounce crème de violette
Dash of absinthe

Coat a cocktail glass with absinthe. In a mixing glass, add the gin, vermouth, crème de violette and ice. Stir and strain into the coated cocktail glass.

SIDECAR

The Sidecar made its first appearance in Paris at the end of World War I. An American Army captain who was being chauffeured around town in a motorcycle's sidecar had a cold and wasn't feeling well. Before dinner, the captain asked to stop at a café where he asked the bartender to fix him a drink that would make him feel better.

In that era, brandy was sometimes used as a medicine, though it was usually served as an after-dinner drink. Before-dinner drinks are usually lighter and contain a citrus to stir the appetite.

The clever bartender decided to kill two birds with one stone and combined brandy and lemon juice to help the captain's cold and build his appetite for dinner. The Sidecar was born.

1½ ounces brandy or cognac
½ ounce lemon juice, freshly squeezed
½ ounce triple sec

Add all the ingredients to a mixing glass. Add ice and shake. Strain into a cocktail glass and garnish with a lemon twist.

U.S. Army motorcycle and sidecar, circa 1917

SPIFICATOR

The Spificator is a simple, yet refreshing cocktail with a name that is pure Cincinnati. I love it! Christopher F. Lawlor came up with the name in his 1895 book, *The Mixicologist*. Lawlor was the head bartender at the Burnet House hotel, located downtown on Third and Vine streets. It was one of the grandest hotels in the United States from 1851 through 1925. Generals Ulysses S. Grant and William Tecumseh Sherman met at the Burnet House to work out plans for victory in the Civil War, and President Abraham Lincoln was once a guest there.

The Spificator is a highball, and the highball was claimed to have been invented by Patrick Duffy, a bartender at the Ashland House in New York City, in 1890. Basically, a highball is a spirit with a carbonated mixer served in a tall glass.

The name *highball* was inspired by the days of train travel. In modern air travel, we have the "fasten seat belt" sign. In Victorian-era train travel, they had the "highball" light. As a train left the station and gained speed, a series of lights would engage to indicate how fast the train was moving. Once the top light, or the highball as it was called, lit up, the train was at top speed, and passengers were free to move to the bar car and enjoy some refreshments. In other words, it was "highball time."

2 ounces brandy
Soda to top

Fill a highball glass with ice. Add the brandy and top off with soda.

BETWEEN THE SHEETS

This cocktail hails back to the days of Prohibition, 1919 through 1933. Life was lived at a much faster and looser pace during that time. Jazzy flappers wore hems higher than polite society approved of, bobbed their hair, painted their lips bright red, and—what may have been the worst infraction of all—drank booze in speakeasies with men.

Garter flasks were the ultimate flapper accessory in the 1920s.

There needed to be a drink that could keep up with this hedonistic era, and Between the Sheets was just the concoction. Two spirits in one drink would either put you between the sheets with someone you loved or land you there all alone, wondering what the heck happened.

1 ounce rum
1 ounce brandy
½ ounce triple sec
½ ounce lemon juice, freshly squeezed

Add all the ingredients and ice to a mixing glass and shake. Strain into a cocktail glass. Garnish with a lemon twist.

AIRMAIL COCKTAIL

This is such a great cocktail! It first appeared in the 1949 cocktail book *Handbook for Hosts*. There isn't much history available about this drink, but the name reminds me of the story of the first unofficial airmail delivery, which took place in my hometown of Cincinnati.

Believe it or not, one of the first unofficial airmail deliveries in the United States occurred in 1835, during an era when mail delivery could take up to several months as letters and packages made their way to their destinations via horseback or stagecoach.

Balloonist Richard Clayton attempted to deliver a package from Cincinnati to the East Coast. Clayton left Cincinnati at 5 P.M. on July 4, 1835. A few hours into the flight, the balloon began to lose altitude, forcing Clayton to jettison some of the provisions in order to lighten the weight. In his desperation to keep the balloon afloat, he even tossed his dog overboard. (Don't panic, dog lovers. Clayton didn't really toss Rover over the side; he used a rope to gently lower the dog to the ground. The rope was found later without the attached pooch, so the assumption was that the dog safely arrived on earth, though it was never seen again.)

By 2 A.M., July 5, Clayton had made it to Keeney's Knob, West Virginia, where the balloon became entangled in a tree. Some local citizens helped Clayton wrestle the balloon out of the tree. The package was sent on by stagecoach to complete its journey, and Clayton returned to Cincinnati via steamboat. Something positive

did come out of Clayton's fiasco: The post office in the town near Keeney's Knob was named after him.

I guess it depends on how many of these cocktails you have as to whether your journey ends at its intended destination.

> 1½ ounces rum
> ½ ounce lime juice, freshly squeezed
> ½ ounce honey simple syrup
> Champagne to top

Add the rum, lime juice, syrup, and ice to a mixing glass and shake. Strain into a champagne flute. Top off with champagne.

Honey Simple Syrup

> 1 cup water
> 1 cup honey

Combine the water and honey in a pan over medium heat. Stir continually until the honey and water are evenly combined.

LIME IN THE COCONUT *(Pictured)*

   1½ ounces rum
   ½ ounce coconut simple syrup
   2 lime wedges
   15 cilantro leaves
   Soda to top

Muddle the lime and cilantro in a mixing glass. Add the rum, syrup, and ice, and shake. Strain into an ice-filled highball glass and top with soda. Garnish with additional cilantro leaves and lime wedges.

Coconut Simple Syrup

   1 cup water
   1 cup sugar
   1 cup shredded coconut flakes

Follow the instructions for making simple syrup in chapter 2.

QUEEN'S PARK SWIZZLE

The Queen's Park Hotel was built in 1895 in Savannah, Trinidad. Located across from the picturesque Queen's Park Savannah, the hotel was the gem of the island and considered the grandest hotel of its time. The Queen's Park Swizzle was created at the hotel in 1920.

The swizzle was first mentioned in print in 1788. The name refers to the way the drink is mixed. It's not shaken or stirred; it's swizzled. Swizzling involves a special stick that has small branches at the end. The stick is placed in the drink with crushed ice and rotated back and forth between the palms of your hands. If you don't have a swizzle stick, a bar spoon will work just fine.

This is one of the most refreshing drinks ever! Lots of ice and plenty of rum make for a perfect drink for a hot summer day.

2 ounces rum
½ ounce triple sec
6–8 mint leaves
3 dashes bitters
½ ounce lime juice, freshly squeezed
Soda to top

In a highball glass, add the mint, rum, lime juice, triple sec, and bitters. Add crushed ice until the glass is half full. Swizzle with a swizzle stick or bar spoon. Add more ice until the cup is full and top off with soda.

DARK AND STORMY

1½ ounces Gosling's rum

½ ounce ginger simple syrup (see chapter 2 for recipe)

Dash of lime juice, freshly squeezed

Soda to top

Add the rum, lime juice, and ginger syrup to a highball glass. Add ice and top off with soda.

OPY *(Pictured)*

1½ ounces rum

½ ounce lime juice, freshly squeezed

½ ounce ginger simple syrup (see chapter 2 for recipe)

½ ounce strawberry puree

Mint leaves

Soda to top

Add all the ingredients to a mixing glass along with ice and shake. Strain into an old fashioned glass filled with ice. Top with soda. Garnish with mint leaves.

CINNAMON ORANGE MARGARITA *(Pictured)*

> 2 ounces Reposado tequila (not Gold)
> 1 ounce orange juice, freshly squeezed
> ½ ounce cinnamon simple syrup

Add all the ingredients and ice to a mixing glass. Shake and strain into a cocktail glass. Garnish with an orange slice dipped in cinnamon.

Cinnamon Simple Syrup

> 1 cup sugar
> 1 cup water
> 1 tablespoon cinnamon

Follow the directions for making simple syrup in chapter 2.

ARMILLITA CHICO

While in Mexico in 1937, Charles H. Baker Jr. created this drink and named it for the most beautiful bullfighter in Mexico, Armillita Chico. Chico (nicknamed Fermin Espinosa Saucedo) was known for his grace and skillfulness. He made $1,500 a day fighting bulls.

Tequila was not a popular mixer in the 1930s; it was normally consumed as a shot in those days. Baker, however, loved cocktails. This cocktail predates the margarita.

A bullfight in Matamoros, Mexico, 1942

1½ ounces tequila

½ ounce lime juice, freshly squeezed

½ ounce grenadine simple syrup (see chapter 2 for recipe)

Dash of orange blossom water

Add all the ingredients and ice to a mixing glass. Shake and strain into a cocktail glass.

* * *

PALOMA

The Paloma is Mexico's favorite tequila cocktail. The fruit juice masks the harshness of the tequila. The first published recipe for this drink is credited to Evan Harrison. *Paloma* is Spanish for dove or pigeon.

1½ ounces tequila

1 ounce grapefruit juice

½ ounce triple sec

Soda to top

Build over ice in a highball glass. Top off with soda and garnish with wheels of lemon, lime, and grapefruit.

PUERTO VALLARTA *(Pictured)*

> 1½ ounces tequila
> ¼ ounce lime juice, freshly squeezed
> ½ ounce Heering Cherry Liqueur
> ½ ounce Bénédictine
> Soda to top

Build over ice in a highball glass. Top with soda. Garnish with a cherry.

HOT TIJUANA NIGHTS *(Pictured)*

    1½ ounces tequila
    1 ounce grapefruit juice, freshly squeezed
    ½ ounce lime juice, freshly squeezed
    ½ ounce jalapeño simple syrup

Add all the ingredients to a mixing glass. Add ice and shake. Strain into an old fashioned glass filled with ice. Garnish with a jalapeño slice.

Jalapeño Simple Syrup

    1 cup sugar
    1 cup water
    1 chopped jalapeño

Follow the directions for making simple syrup in chapter 2.

6

DRINKS WITH DINNER

PAIRING FOOD WITH COCKTAILS is just as delicious and enjoyable as pairing food with wine or beer. I've enjoyed working with the most amazing chefs in Cincinnati and in many restaurants to craft cocktails to complement their culinary creations. When you pair with cocktails, you have more flavor pairing options to explore. Try pairing your main dish with a cocktail at your next dinner party or brunch. It makes your dining experience that much better.

REMEMBER THE MAINE

When American food writer and world traveler Charles H. Baker Jr. reached Havana, Cuba, in 1933, he had no idea he would be spending more time there than originally planned. It seems he wandered right into the middle of a revolution.

The dictator at the time was Machado, a poor excuse for a man and not much of a dictator either. He bribed Cuba's congress to receive a second term in office. The country was already in the midst of a great depression, and he further mismanaged the government dealings so badly, including the country's business with America, that the people staged a revolt in protest.

Seeking safety in his hotel room, Baker observed the chaos in the city. He was inspired to create something to memorialize this event. Though he was a writer by trade, he didn't want to use words for this tribute. He wanted something different, and then it came to him: A cocktail would be a wonderful way to remember the

The wrecked USS *Maine*, Havana Cuba, circa 1903

Cuban uprising. The name came to him immediately: Remember the Maine, a popular slogan in the United States during the Spanish-American War. The sinking of the USS *Maine* in 1889 provoked the Spanish-American War, and Baker imagined the fighting he saw in Havana must have been similar to the fighting during the earlier conflict. Yes, he thought it a fitting tribute: *Remember the* Maine ... *to hell with Spain*!

 1½ ounces rye
 ½ ounce Heering Cherry Liqueur
 ½ ounce sweet vermouth
 ¼ ounce absinthe

Coat a cocktail glass with the absinthe. In a mixing glass, add the rye, Heering Cherry, and sweet vermouth. Add ice, stir, and strain into the coated cocktail glass.

* * *

PORTER CUP

 1 ounce port
 1 ounce brandy
 2 ounces ale/beer
 ½ ounce ginger simple syrup (see chapter 2 for recipe)

Add the port, brandy, and ginger syrup to a mixing glass. Add ice and shake. Strain into a rocks glass. Top off with ale and garnish with a sprinkle of grated nutmeg and a slice of cucumber.

APPLE OF MY ISLAY *(Pictured)*

    1½ ounces scotch
    ¼ ounce lemon juice, freshly squeezed
    ½ ounce apple simple syrup
    1 ounce IPA beer

Add the scotch, lemon juice, and apple syrup to a mixing glass. Add ice and shake. Strain into a small rocks glass and top with beer. Garnish with an apple wedge.

Apple Simple Syrup

    1 cup sugar
    1 cup water
    1 apple, sliced

Follow the directions for making simple syrup in chapter 2.

LITTLE BOY BLUE *(Pictured)*

2 ounces bourbon
2 ounces blueberry simple syrup
Stout to top

Add the bourbon and blueberry syrup to a mixing glass. Add ice and shake. Strain into a small rocks glass. Top with stout. Garnish with blueberries.

Blueberry Simple Syrup

1 cup sugar
1 cup water
½ cup fresh or frozen blueberries

Follow the directions for making simple syrup in chapter 2.

CORNUCOPIA COCKTAIL *(Pictured)*

> 1½ ounces bourbon
> ½ ounce wine simple syrup
> ½ ounce lime juice, freshly squeezed
> Dash of allspice bitters (see chapter 2 for recipe)

Add all the ingredients to a mixing glass. Add ice and shake. Strain into a cocktail glass.

Wine Simple Syrup

> 1 cup sugar
> 1 cup red wine

Follow the directions for making simple syrup in chapter 2, substituting red wine for water.

BRUNSWICK SOUR *(Pictured)*

1½ ounces rum
½ ounce triple sec
½ ounce lime juice, freshly squeezed
½ ounce red wine

Add the rum, triple sec, and lime juice to a rocks glass. Fill with ice and stir. Top with red wine.

* * *

NEGRONI

An Italian count and a rodeo clown—you couldn't find a more unlikely combination, and yet they come together in the backstory of this drink.

It was 1919. Count Camillo Negroni of Florence was enjoying an Americano, a mix of Campari and soda, but he felt the drink wasn't quite right. Instead of more soda, it needed something to fire it up—gin. So the Negroni is an Americano with an extra shot of gin.

Most people serve this cocktail as a before-dinner drink. Campari is an Italian aperitif. It wakes up your taste buds and gets you ready to eat. Gaspare Campari developed the liqueur in the 1860s. It's a fusion of fruit, aromatic plants, and bitter herbs. The liqueur's bright red color often creates an expectation of an overly sweet concoction, but it has a citrus taste with a bitter but bright follow-up.

Continued

Let me leave you with one more interesting point, not about the cocktail, but about our friend, Count Negroni. Remember at the beginning of this story I mentioned that the Negroni has an Italian count and a rodeo clown in its history? Well, while the count lived in America, he earned his living working as a rodeo clown. Odd, but true.

> 1 ounce gin
> 1 ounce sweet vermouth
> 1 ounce Campari

Add all the ingredients to a mixing glass. Add ice and stir until cold. Strain into a cocktail glass.

* * *

GINGER ROGERS *(Pictured)*

> 1½ ounces gin
> ½ ounce lemon juice, freshly squeezed
> ½ ounce ginger simple syrup (see chapter 2 for recipe)
> Wheat beer to top

Add the gin, lemon juice, and ginger syrup to a mixing glass. Add ice and shake. Strain into a rocks glass. Top off with the wheat beer. Garnish with a piece of ginger.

HARVEST MOON *(Pictured)*

1½ ounces gin
1 ounce Lillet
½ ounce saffron honey simple syrup
Dash of orange bitters (see chapter 2 for recipe)

Add all the ingredients to a mixing glass. Add ice and shake. Strain into a cocktail glass. Garnish with an orange twist.

Saffron Honey Simple Syrup

1 cup honey
1 cup water
½ teaspoon saffron threads

Follow the directions for making simple syrup in chapter 2, substituting honey for sugar.

ICHABOD CRANE *(Pictured)*

    1½ ounces Reposado tequila
    1 ounce pumpkin simple syrup
    ½ ounce vanilla simple syrup (see chapter 2 for recipe)

Add all the ingredients to a mixing glass. Add ice and shake. Strain into a cocktail glass. Garnish with a sprinkle of nutmeg.

Pumpkin Simple Syrup

    1 cup sugar
    1 cup water
    ½ cup pumpkin puree
    Dash of cinnamon

Follow the directions for making simple syrup in chapter 2.

BEET AROUND THE CHRISTMAS TREE *(Pictured)*

2 ounces tequila

1 ounce fresh beet juice

½ ounce lemon juice, freshly squeezed

¾ ounce vanilla simple syrup (see chapter 2 for recipe)

Soda to top

Add everything but the soda to a mixing glass. Add ice and shake. Strain over ice into an old fashioned glass. Top with soda and garnish with a rosemary sprig.

7

AFTER-DINNER DRINKS

A DIGESTIF IS A LIQUEUR served after dinner to aid digestion. Many of these liqueurs contain herbs that reduce bloat from eating a heavy meal. Sherry, vermouth, port, madeira, and brandy are all common digestifs.

An after-dinner drink is also a nice way to relax during the evening. Warm drinks are calming and comforting, which is a great way to wrap up your night.

APPLE BUTTER TODDY *(Pictured)*

2 ounces bourbon
2 bar spoons of apple butter
2 bar spoons of vanilla simple syrup (see chapter 2 for recipe)
Dash of allspice bitters (see chapter 2 for recipe)
Hot water to top

In a heat-resistant glass (such as a mug), add the bourbon, apple butter, and vanilla syrup, and stir. Add bitters. Top with hot water and stir. Garnish with an apple wedge and cinnamon stick.

* * *

COMFY COUCH

Tuaca is a brandy-based liqueur with orange and vanilla flavoring.

1½ ounces bourbon
½ ounce Tuaca liqueur
1 ounce port

Build over ice in an old fashioned glass.

BLACK STALLION *(Pictured)*

1½ ounces bourbon
½ ounce crème de cacao
Dash of cayenne bitters
Stout to top

Add the bourbon, crème de cacao, and cayenne bitters to a mixing glass. Add ice and shake. Strain into a rocks glass. Top with stout.

Cayenne Bitters

2 cups vodka
1 fresh cayenne pepper chopped, or 1 tablespoon cayenne
    pepper powder
Zest from 1 lemon
Pith from one lemon
3 mason jars with lids

Equally divide the vodka between the 3 mason jars. Add the cayenne to one jar, the lemon zest to one jar, and the pith to the last jar. Seal with the lids. Let the jars sit for 1 week at room temperature, shaking each jar daily. At the end of the week, combine all of the liquids into one jar. Shake and then taste. (Take a small taste as it's very spicy.) It should have a very spicy taste with an undertone of the lemon. Strain and bottle.

I'M A NUT

1½ ounces bourbon

½ ounce walnut liqueur

1 bar spoon of chocolate syrup

Hot coffee to top

Add the bourbon, walnut liqueur, and chocolate syrup to a coffee cup and stir. Top with hot coffee and stir.

* * *

COCO COOL *(Pictured)*

2 ounces whiskey

½ ounce chocolate syrup

6 mint leaves

1 ounce stout beer

Add the whiskey, chocolate syrup, and mint leaves to a mixing glass. Add ice and shake. Strain into a rocks glass. Top with stout and garnish with an additional sprig of mint.

SMOKEHOUSE *(Pictured)*

　　1½ ounces scotch
　　½ ounce vanilla simple syrup (see chapter 2 for recipe)
　　Dash of tobacco bitters
　　1 piece of ginger root

Muddle the ginger and tobacco bitters together in a mixing glass. Add the scotch, vanilla syrup, and ice and shake. Double strain into a cocktail glass. Garnish with a piece of ginger.

RUSTY NAIL

The Rusty Nail is an iconic cocktail made famous in the 1960s by the Rat Pack. It uses Drambuie, a whiskey liqueur with a colorful history from the Isle of Skye in Scotland. According to legend, Bonnie Prince Charlie gave the original recipe to some Highland clans in 1746. In 1873, John Ross began making the liqueur and serving it in his hotel, The Broadford, on Skye. It grew in popularity, and commercial bottling started in 1909. According to the makers, the name is a shortened version of the Gaelic phrase *an dram buidheach*, which means "the drink that satisfies."

2 ounces scotch

½ ounce Drambuie liqueur

Build over ice in an old fashioned glass. Garnish with a lemon twist.

* * *

YOGI BEAR

Birch beer is a carbonated nonalcoholic drink similar to root beer. It's a nice complement to the anise flavor of the absinthe.

1½ ounces absinthe

3 ounces birch beer

Build over ice in an old fashioned glass.

HANKY PANKY

This cocktail was created by one of the most famous female bartenders in the business, Ada Coleman. Her nickname was Coley, and she mixed cocktails at the famous American Bar at the Savoy Hotel in London from 1903 to 1926. She could hold her own when engaging with her guests and could trash-talk with the best of them.

She created the Hanky Panky for Savoy regular Charles Hawtrey, an English actor. One day Hawtrey came into the bar needing a drink with a punch to it. Coley mixed up a cocktail featuring three spirits, and after downing a few, Hawtrey exclaimed, "By jove! Now that was a hanky panky." The name stuck, and it has been a Hanky Panky ever since.

This cocktail features Fernet, a type of Italian amaro made from forty different herbs and spices. Fernet is commonly served after dinner with coffee to aid digestion. It can be an acquired taste, but once you have developed an appreciation for Fernet, you'll enjoy it in many cocktails.

1 ounce gin
1 ounce sweet vermouth
1 ounce Fernet

Add all the ingredients to a mixing glass. Add ice and stir. Strain into a cocktail glass.

INDEX

DEDICATION
To my family.

And to everyone in Cincinnati to whom I've had the pleasure of serving a drink.

ABOUT THE AUTHOR
Molly Wellmann is a self-taught mixologist and co-owner of Japp's, Japp's Annex, Neons, and the Old Kentucky Bourbon Bar in Cincinnati, Ohio. She was voted best mixologist/bartender in Cincinnati by *CityBeat* magazine in 2010, 2011, and 2012. Molly has been featured in *The New York Times*, *The Cincinnati Enquirer*, *Cincinnati* magazine and *The Washington Post*.

presented herein. It is the purchaser's responsibility to read and follow all instructions and warnings on all product labels. Published by Betterway Home Books, an imprint of F+W Media, Inc., 10151 Carver Rd., Suite 200, Blue Ash, Ohio, 45242. (800) 289-0963. First Edition.

ISBN: 978-1-4403-3009-4

Other fine Betterway Home Books are available from your local bookstore or online or direct from the publisher. Visit our website, www.betterwaybooks.com.

17   16   15   5   4   3

Distributed in Canada by Fraser Direct
100 Armstrong Avenue, Georgetown, Ontario, Canada L7G 5S4,
Tel: (905) 877-4411

Distributed in the U.K. and Europe by F&W Media International, LTD
Brunel House, Forde Close, Newton Abbot, TQ12 4PU, UK, Tel: (+44) 1626 323200,
Fax: (+44) 1626 323319, E-mail: enquiries@fwmedia.com

Distributed in Australia by Capricorn Link
P.O. Box 704, S. Windsor NSW, 2756 Australia, Tel: (02) 4560-1600,
Fax: (02) 4577-5288, E-mail: books@capricornlink.com.au

Edited by Jacqueline Musser
Designed by Clare Finney
Photography by Al Parrish unless otherwise noted
Production coordinated by Debbie Thomas

MORE TO IMBIBE!

Making Wine with Fruits,
Roots & Flowers
By Margaret Crowther

To Drink or Not to Drink
By Adams Media

Bartender's Guide:
An A to Z Companion to
All Your Favorite Drinks
By John K. Waters

AVAILABLE ONLINE AND IN BOOKSTORES EVERYWHERE!

To get started join our mailing list at betterwaybooks.com.

Become a fan of our Facebook page:
facebook.com/BetterwayHomeBooks

OTR *(Pictured)*

This is my twist on a vodka cranberry. I named this drink in honor of Over-the-Rhine, the Cincinnati neighborhood where Japp's is located. The entire neighborhood (more than 900 buildings) is in the National Register of Historic Places, and the building exteriors haven't changed much since they were built in the mid-1800s by a large German immigrant population. Originally, the Miami and Erie Canal separated the neighborhood from downtown Cincinnati, and the city's residents nicknamed the canal the Rhine because of the German immigrants. The canal was eventually filled in (Central Parkway sits atop it now), but the name remains.

1½ ounces vodka
1 ounce cranberry juice
½ ounces vanilla simply syrup (see chapter 2 for recipe)
Dash of rose water

Add all the ingredients to a mixing glass. Add ice and shake. Strain into a cocktail glass. Garnish with a rose petal if desired.

The Miami and Erie Canal once separated the neighborhood of Over-the-Rhine from downtown Cincinnati.

SAZERAC

Peychaud's Bitters was created in the 1830s by a French-Haitian man named Antoine Amédée Peychaud. He fled from Haiti to New Orleans in the early 1800s following battles between French troops and black slaves who desired freedom. Peychaud opened an apothecary at 437 Royal Street in the French Quarter and began making a bitters formula that he had learned in Haiti.

Peychaud became known for his Sazerac toddy, which was made with Sazerac brand cognac, sugar, Peychaud's own bitters, and an anisette. This drink was served in an egg-shaped cup called a coquetier (pronounced cock-a-tiay). Some say the coquetier gave rise to the name *cocktail*, but there are many stories that claim to be the origin of the cocktail (so many that they could fill another book).

In the 1870s, the rights to Peychaud's Bitters were sold to New Orleans bartender Thomas H. Handy, who continued making the Sazerac, but used rye instead of cognac.

> 2 ounces rye
> 1 sugar cube
> ½ ounce absinthe
> 3 dashes Peychaud's Bitters

Coat a cocktail glass with absinthe. Add the sugar cube and bitters to a mixing glass and muddle. Add the rye and ice and stir until cold. Strain into the coated cocktail glass.